Christmas details

Christmas details

Mary Norden

photography by **Sandra Lane**

RYLAND
PETERS
& SMALL
London New York

*To the Garrads, for all the
wonderful Christmasses*

Designer Sally Powell
Senior editor Annabel Morgan
Recipe editor Maddalena Bastianelli
Location research Kate Brunt
Production Meryl Silbert
Publishing director Alison Starling
Art director Gabriella Le Grazie

Stylist Mary Norden
Recipes Kathy Man

First published in Great Britain in 2000 by
Ryland Peters & Small
Cavendish House
51–55 Mortimer Street
London WIN 7TD

1 3 5 7 9 10 8 6 4 2

ISBN 1 84172 080 1

A CIP catalogue record for this book is available from the British Library.

Printed and bound in China by Toppan Printing Co.

contents

introduction

*T*he clue to a successful Christmas lies in the title to this book –
attention to detail is all-important. Within these pages you'll
find plenty of inspiration for decorating ideas, grouped in different
themes to help you plan a coordinated look, whether you want a
country-style Christmas or a contemporary one. There are new ideas for
traditional festive elements, such as candles and wreaths, and
even alternative Christmas trees for modern interiors. You'll
also find instructions for elegant handmade cards, ingenious
ways to wrap presents, recipes for homebaked goodies, and
pretty table settings. Most of the ideas are inexpensive, all are
extremely simple. These elegant and imaginative details will
help you celebrate the festive season with style and make
it truly special for you, your family and your friends.
Happy Christmas!

decorative themes

white christmas

For a white Christmas that doesn't rely on the weather, use pristine materials and simple decorative details to create a sophisticated scheme for house and table. Gather together white paper, bleached stones, creamy candles and milky, translucent glass. Look around haberdashery departments for furnishing trims and unusual materials that will give your scheme an original edge. Remember that as you are not using colour or pattern, texture will play a more important role.

This page and opposite: Pompom braid – sold by the metre to edge cushions and curtains – can be cut into short lengths and used to secure rolled napkins instead of a traditional ring. Alternatively, place a chalky white stone trimmed with fine silver cord atop a folded napkin. Repeat the theme by adding more pebbles along the length of the table.

setting the scene

There's something very decadent about feathers.

Use them to trim napkin rings, made from

equally glamorous sequinned braid, and

to fashion a soft, fluffy, festive wreath.

Opposite: Roll up stiffly starched damask napkins and secure with strips of sequinned braid or other tactile trimmings. Tuck a feather into each one.

Right: Milky glass beakers stand on a length of intricate, handmade Japanese paper embossed with circles. Use unusual paper as a table runner or, alternatively, cut it into rectangles and use as table mats.

Left: A snowy place setting is composed of all-white elements with a variety of different textures, from the smooth glass beaker to the crisp damask napkin and the fragile Japanese paper.

Left: A festive feather wreath is easy to make. Use a wire coat hanger and snip off the hook with pliers or, if you prefer, retain it to hang the wreath from. Buy a cheap feather boa and secure one end to the wreath base with a twist of fine wire or tape and then just wind the feathers round. Tuck in the end and leave the wreath plain or add silver baubles and bows. Hang on a door using a loop of white satin ribbon, or hook casually over a chair, as shown here.

white winter boughs

You don't have to go without a Christmas tree just because a traditional fir won't suit a simple white decorating scheme. Instead, reinvent the tree for a modern interior, using bold graphic lines and plain frosted baubles.

Above: Rather than hanging fairy lights from the branches, think of other ways to use them, such as winding them round the pot that holds the willow boughs.
Right: Resist the urge to add gaudy coloured baubles. Cool, frosted shapes enhance branches lightly dusted with white.

For a totally modern effect, complement a restrained white scheme with an understated 'tree' made from branches of twisted willow. Contorted willow or hazel branches are available from florists. To give them a subtle dusting of white, spray them lightly with white spray paint. Stand the branches in a galvanized metal bucket and use scrunched-up newspaper, pebbles or sand to hold them upright. For a strictly white theme, wrap presents in pristine white tissue paper and tie them with frosty white or silver ribbon.

Above: Intriguing decorations are made by cutting stars from silver or white card and slipping them inside tiny greaseproof-paper envelopes. Other shapes also work well.
Left: These tiny, fleecy white baby socks secured with café clips make enchanting and unusual tree decorations.

white

Above: Instead of
candlesticks, use small white
porcelain bowls. Fix candles
to the base with blu-tac
then surround with gravel.
Right: Use a glass vase filled
with white gravel (available
from garden centres) to
hold the tapers. For real
drama, set them in a big
galvanized metal bucket.

16

pure and simple candles

Candles may be centuries old, but they can be used in strikingly contemporary

ways. Mass a handful of tall, thin tapers together in a vase or bucket, group

stout church candles on mantelpieces or table centres, and fill the festive

home with the inimitable warm and welcoming glow of candlelight.

Left and below: A massed group of candles of varying heights and thicknesses creates a generous and dramatic effect. If you can stand the candles before a reflective surface, such as a glass wall or window, so much the better. This arrangement would work equally well on a mantelpiece with a mirror behind it, or ranged down the centre of a dining table. Surrounding the candles with large chalky white pebbles adds textural interest.

pretty packages

Wrapping small gifts stylishly (rather like wedding favours), means you can also use them as part of your table decorations. Make the gifts an integral component of each place setting – you could even label each one so they double up as name cards – or hand them round yourself after dinner.

The Christmas table offers an ideal opportunity to present tiny tokens with maximum impact. Even the simplest gifts can look glamorous with a little thought and preparation. Swathes of white tissue paper soon turn a chocolate into an exotic flower, while a ceramic dish can elevate a handful of sweets into an elegant dinner-table adornment. Equally stylish presentation can be used when serving some of the food too, from wrapping a warm dinner roll in a napkin to smartly packaging after-dinner mints or biscuits for coffee.

Right: Small white ceramic bowls filled with bonbons, with their characteristic dusting of icing sugar, and finished with a silky white cord make thoughtful place settings and covetable small Christmas gifts too.

Opposite: Chocolates laid on squares of pristine white tissue paper gathered with delicate organza ribbon, can be handed round with dessert to be eaten at the table or even taken home instead as a party favour.

white

Opposite: A bread roll wrapped in a napkin and tied with white cord is ready and waiting for dinner to begin. **Right:** Serve after-dinner coffee with individually wrapped mints, parcelled in white card with a twist of ribbon. **Below**: Write guests' names on white labels, thread them on to a length of white cord and tie round two or three breadsticks for an unusual appetizer that doubles up as a place card.

Presenting food stylishly pleases the eye as well as whetting the appetite.

traditional christmas

By using your imagination and thinking a little more widely, you can come up with a reassuringly traditional Christmas scheme that doesn't just fall back on good old holly and ivy for decoration. Extend the colour palette beyond the traditional berry-scarlet, instead bringing opulent shades of maroon and purplish black into play. Instead of plain green leaves, include hints of copper foliage and the gleam of silver, and use these rich, regal colours to decorate both table and tree, incorporating seasonal fruits and flowers wherever you can.

Opposite, above and left: Contrast the purple bloom of ripe figs with the deep velvety hue of red roses. Pile the fruit on a platter then scatter rose heads casually between the pieces. Cut the flower stems just before you arrange them, and they should last for the rest of the day.

23

Right, far right and opposite: Claret-red ribbon, coppery foliage and a sprig of berries can be fashioned into a smart napkin ring. Try substituting a small bunch of red grapes for the berries or, for true luxury, rose heads.

decorating the table

Christmas dinner is one of the most important meals of the year and should be prepared for accordingly. Taking the time to plan and set a beautiful table shows guests how much you care, and contributes enormously to the sense of occasion.

If you have a fine oak or dark wood table, leave it uncovered so that the rich, dark gleam of the wood is included in the overall scheme (you may want to use individual place mats to protect the table from hot dishes). Create a simple but effective centrepiece for the table using a glass cake stand piled high with an assortment of luscious fruits and extravagant red roses. Continue the strong and sumptuous colour scheme by making your own napkin rings from lengths of crimson silk ribbon, a handful of fresh leaves and a sprig of ruby-red translucent berries.

Right: A traditional-style
Christmas tree can take
plenty of decorations, but
resist the urge to overdo
things or you will conceal
the shape and colour of the
tree itself. Here, baubles of
three different sizes but in
the same shade of rich
scarlet have been
supplemented with tiny
white crackers, fairy lights
and the occasional discreet
sparkle of gold.

When choosing a Christmas tree, look for one that looks healthy and is a good shape. Shake gently; if needles fall off, the tree won't last well.

dressing the tree

The popularity of the Christmas tree in Britain is due almost entirely to Prince Albert, whose enthusiasm for decorating them caught on in the mid-nineteenth century. Today we can choose from six or seven different species, with needles in a variety of green shades.

Above: Make miniature crackers to decorate the Christmas tree, choosing colours that echo those on the dining table. Roll up a piece of card (place a gift inside, if you like) and tape in place. Cover the roll with a piece of white crepe paper that is about 15cm longer than the tube. Tie each end with ribbon and a sprig of berries. Lay the crackers on the tree branches.
Left: Rich red baubles (suspended from silky red twine) gleam in the warm glow cast by tiny fairy lights.

Right: Punctuate the basic
wreath with clusters of
brighter red fake berries.
These come on soft wire
stems and can easily be
attached to the original
wreath at intervals around
the circumference. Add a
plain red velvet streamer to
match the new berries and
hang the wreath over a
door. If you don't want to
damage the paintwork
and there's a convenient
coat hook on the other
side of the door, hang the
wreath on invisible fishing
line and loop it right over
the top of the door.

ringing the changes

A ready-made wreath of artificial berries will last for years. Make it appear
fresh and different each Christmas by dressing it with new accessories and
using it in a variety of different ways – propped on a mantelpiece, as part of
a candle arrangement or, in time-honoured tradition, to decorate a door.

Left: Tie bows from red satin ribbon and slightly narrower
tartan ribbon and wire them in pairs to your basic berry
wreath for a pretty and colourful combination, ideal for
the end of a mantelpiece or a sheltered front door.
Above: Weaving stems of fresh ivy through the wreath
creates a more natural effect. On this hall shelf, three
wreaths encircle groups of candles to create a dramatic
welcome. Varying the height of the candles stops the effect
from looking overly contrived. This arrangement would
work just as well on a mantelpiece or a deep windowsill.

hanging decorations

Simple decorations are often the most charming. Greenery hung from door handles and chair backs brings Christmas cheer to every room in the house.

Hanging decorations can be made from whatever comes to hand: a few trimmings from the Christmas tree, a handful of berries – artificial or real – or spare baubles, preferably unbreakable. If you are using greenery for door-handle decorations, hang them on a generous loop of ribbon so that you don't get pricked every time you reach for the handle. Don't forget fresh flowers, too. Red roses are available all year round and team beautifully with berries and evergreen leaves.

Above and right: Wind ivy on to a thin wire ring, add a few red rose heads and hang from a length of matching velvet ribbon.
Far right: Glue dried seedheads to a polystyrene ball and hang with ribbon for a robust decoration.
Opposite: A posy of fir and berries tied with red ribbon.

clever candleholders

Ordinary household items such as tea-glass holders

or empty jam jars can be given a new lease of life

as candleholders. With a little imagination, even

the most mundane objects have new potential.

Look round the house and you will find some unusual and appealing candleholders, such as these glass yogurt pots, which have a very pretty shape and need minimal decoration to transform them from discarded to desirable. If you are worried about the glass cracking as the candle burns down, pour a little water into the bottom of the pots. Whatever your candleholder, make sure the candle is fixed firmly upright (blu-tac is useful) and keep an eye on them as they burn down, particularly when using foliage and berries to decorate them.

Right: A twist of ivy and a couple of beaded berries transform a glass yogurt pot into a pretty candle-holder. It will also catch any dripping wax.

Above and opposite: The silver bases that hold Russian tea glasses also make perfect candle containers. Fill them with a handful of ivy leaves and berries and range a row of them along a mantelpiece or running the length of your dining table.

When used as candleholders, these old glass yogurt pots are transformed from discarded to desirable.

exotic
christmas

To set the scene for an exotic Christmas, turn

to the riches of the East. The three kings,

with their jewelled turbans and brocade robes,

carrying gifts of gold, frankincense and

myrrh, inspire a colour scheme of burgundy

and maroon shot through with metallic

thread, beaded decorations and curtains of

stars. Heady perfumes and aromatics translate

into spicy pomanders and exotic sweetmeats.

This page and opposite: A circular mirror makes a beautiful and practical base for a candle arrangement, reflecting the glow of the flames and protecting the surface below from wax at the same time. Use tree candle clips to hold small candles round the edge of the mirror, place a large scented candle in the centre and surround it with baubles in precious metal colours.

creating the atmosphere

Break away from the traditional Christmas colours of crimson and green and instead imbue your home with the rich hues, warmth and opulence of a more exotic time and place.

For an exotic Christmas, gather together the most sumptuous elements you can find – punched and engraved brass plates that gleam like dull gold, richly coloured and decorated glassware and velvet or tapestry floor cushions. The overall effect should be opulent, bold and very exotic, using lots of burnished gold and jewel-like colours to create a distinctly Moorish feel.

Opposite and left: Exotic kumquats are served in a fluted amber glass bowl.
Far left: A brass plate glints golden in the candlelight. It holds sweetmeats made from dried fruit, nuts and spices – suitably exotic fare.

Opposite and below:
Display the pomanders on
a suitable container – in
this case an engraved metal
Moroccan tray on legs.

spicy pomanders

**The tang of oranges mingling with the piquant
scent of cloves is an unmistakably festive smell.
Home-made pomanders not only smell delicious
but can be decorative too. They also make great
gifts. Follow these tips to create your own designs.**

When oranges are studded with cloves, they are
transformed into pomanders, made the same way since
medieval times. Orange peel can be tough, so prick out
your design first with a darning needle then push the
cloves into the holes. Tie the finished pomanders with a
loop of ribbon and hang from window catches and door
handles. Alternatively, range them along a mantelpiece,
scattered among candles, where the warmth from the
flames will intensify their scent.

Right: As well as trimming gift bags, beads can add a sparkle to all kinds of unexpected objects. Here, an old-fashioned wire cake rack is turned into a festive tray by adding a fringe of jewel-coloured glass beads. For each large bead, you will need a small bead to act as a 'plug' and hold it in place. Thread a needle, knot the end of the thread to the cake rack and pass it through the larger bead then the smaller one. Loop the thread around the outside of the small bead then back through the large bead. Loop thread around the wire rack and continue.

beads, baubles and jewels

The possibilities for decorating with beads are unlimited. Stitch them to fabrics, thread

them on fine wire or simply display handfuls in glass bowls and jars – they look

beautiful just as they are. Look for necklaces of real glass beads in junk shops

or on market stalls, recycle broken necklaces or buy beads from specialist shops.

Drawstring gift bags make ideal packaging for small presents and look especially glamorous when trimmed with delicate, sparkling glass beads. To make a bag, cut two pieces of silk, each 18cm x 18cm. Place the fabric right sides together, and stitch around three sides, leaving one side open. Turn the bag right side out and hem the open top. Just below the hem, stitch two parallel lines to form a channelled drawstring casing, leaving it open at each side. Thread a length of cord through the channel twice and knot the ends. Pull the cord away from both sides of the bag to close it. To decorate your bag, choose beads that complement the colour of the silk. This bag was trimmed with beaded tassels; use your imagination to devise other designs.

Above left: Opulent gold-coloured cutlery is wrapped in a pristine linen napkin and tied with beaded cord.
Above centre: An old-fashioned glass sweet jar is ideal for displaying beaded baubles that look just as precious as finely crafted jewellery.
Above right: Scraps of exquisitely beaded braid or embroidered ribbon won't be wasted if you use them to embellish plain Christmas tree baubles. Carefully remove the bauble's metal neck and wire loop. Fix the ribbon or braid around the circumference of the bauble, using either strong glue or double-sided tape if the decoration is temporary. Replace the wire loop and neck to cover any untidy ends. To give decorated baubles as gifts, leave one at each individual table setting, perhaps attached to a napkin.
Opposite: This collection of glass beads displayed in an old amber-tinted glass seem every bit as exotic and glittery as true gemstones.

A collection of richly coloured glass beads displayed in an old amber-tinted glass seem every bit as exotic and glittery as true gemstones.

festive wreath

A ready-made twig wreath is the base for a whole range of different Christmas designs. Adorn it with greenery for the duration of the holidays or make it into a long-lasting ornament, as shown here.

A ready-made twig wreath is the basis for a festive wreath decorated with tiny parcels and a scattering of stars.

To make this wreath, you will need a ready-made twig wreath, gold spray paint, gold wrapping paper, gold ribbon, small stock cubes and a length of gold wire studded with stars (or similar). Lay the wreath on newspaper and spray with gold paint (two or three light coats are better than one heavy coat). Leave to dry while you wrap the stock cubes in gold paper to look like tiny parcels. Tie each cube with ribbon. Use a hot glue gun or strong adhesive to attach the parcels to the wreath at regular intervals. Finish by winding the starry gold wire round the wreath and tucking in the ends.

45

table decorations

In exotic shades of burgundy and bronze with hints of olive green, this sophisticated table shimmers in the candlelight. The rich colours and the simplicity of the decoration makes a welcome change from the ubiquitous Christmas colours of red and green.

Burgundy and bronze vintage sari fabric makes an unusual and eye-catching runner for this pared-down yet exotic Christmas table. The colours are picked up in the distressed gilt baubles lined up along the length of the table and in the small baubles used to decorate the napkins. Chunky candles complete the look.

Above: Filled with small white candles that stand amid a sea of bronze baubles, this white china cake stand forms a pretty centrepiece that casts a warm glow over the table.
Right and far right: Vintage sari fabric makes a richly coloured runner.

This page: Tie rolled napkins loosely with ribbon and thread on a couple of small baubles that coordinate with the rest of the table setting.

To make the stars you will need delicate gold paper, acetate film and nylon fishing line. Before you cut out the stars, glue the paper to the acetate to reinforce it. Once cut out, the stars are then threaded on lengths of fishing line. Thread the line onto a needle and push the needle through the top and bottom of each star. Make a knot below each star to stop it slipping down. Suspend the strings of stars from nails or drawing pins.

curtain of stars

Suspend a shower of gold stars across a doorway or window to create the most festive curtain imaginable, using the most inexpensive materials.

Opposite, left and above:
Any kind of paper can be used for the stars, but this lacy gold paper creates a particularly ethereal effect.

sparkling votives

Humble nightlights are cheerful and cheap enough to mass together in generous quantities. They are invaluable at Christmas, when they can be scattered on tables, mantelpieces and sideboards.

Instead of placing nightlights in votive glasses, why not jazz up their tin containers with a clever trick or two? Cut sparkly lace braid or another decorative trim into lengths that are slightly longer than the circumference of each nightlight, overlap the two ends and fix the braid neatly in place with glue or double-sided tape. As you won't be constrained by price, mass the nightlights by the dozen on flat mirrors, metal platters and trays. As well as lace braid, you could experiment with plush velvet ribbon, sequinned trim and beaded braid.

Above: Metallic braid with a delicate scalloped edge deceives the eye into thinking that these nightlights are held in filigree metal votives, an illusion further enhanced by placing them on a dull gold platter.

Right and opposite: Introduce a touch of silver to the table by tying napkins with thick silver cord. In keeping with this sleek, contemporary look, fasten with a chunky knot rather than a bow.
Below: Lime-green baubles and fairy lights add sparkle to place settings.

contemporary christmas

Modern metallics set the tone for a completely contemporary Christmas. Mix shades of silver, pewter and dazzling white with occasional flashes of strong, vivid colour for a clean, modern look. Using unusual papers and ribbons is one of the easiest ways to bring metallic effects into the home.

modern metallics

A contemporary Christmas offers an opportunity to break away from tradition. Take inspiration from oriental-style dining and feast at a low-level table.

This setting continues the Far Eastern theme, with simple grey silk table mats placed diagonally and overhanging the table edges, and decoration pared down to just two elements – white fairy lights and baubles.

This page and opposite: Surprise guests with a
skein of fairy lights at the table and a scattering
of shiny baubles to enhance pure white china
and plain, understated glassware.

With a little imagination,
unusual papers can be used to
create unique table settings
that don't cost a fortune.

Paper is enormously useful when decorating the Christmas table. Specialist stationers and high-street stores sell a vast range of unusual papers, and with a little imagination they can be used to create unique table settings that don't cost a fortune. Crinkled paper with a leathery texture makes ideal table mats. Longer lengths could run across the table, linking one place setting to its opposite number. And a roll of wrapping paper would make an elegant runner, stretching from one end of the table to the other.

Above: A collection of frosted and engraved baubles piled high in a fragile glass bowl makes a suitably silvery and shimmery centrepiece for a marvellously modern meal.

Opposite and left: Richly textured silver paper has been cut into squares to create unusual table mats. Instead of fairy lights, a row of tiny votives runs the whole length of the table. Each guest has two napkins that have been starched, folded and laid to form a neat cross. As well as looking decorative, two napkins are a practical note for an extended Christmas dinner with several different courses.

A place mat of folded metallic paper combined with crockery that is similar in feel creates a thoroughly modern table setting.

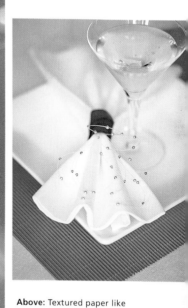

Above: Textured paper like
the silver corrugated square
shown here makes ideal
table mats. Fold strips into
matching napkin rings.
Opposite: Pleat thick paper
into concertinaed table
mats (it should crease easily
without the need for
scoring). The bronze
wallpaper shown here is a
perfect match for the dull
pewter beaker and plate.
Left: To decorate napkins,
keep your eyes open for
off-beat tree decorations
like this airy construction
of wire and beads.

novel napkins

Instead of using conventional napkin rings, create

your own using a medley of different sized,

shaped and coloured ribbons and cords. Keep to

metallic shades and finishes to maintain the theme

but tie each napkin differently to add to the fun.

Opposite and left: Damask napkins are tied with a selection of braids, ribbons and cords, all reflecting a shiny metallic theme.
Below: A roll of pleated metallic ribbon can be cut into lengths to wrap napkins with panache. Add a strip of sequinned braid – choose square-cut or round sequins with an understated matt finish rather than the usual gloss.

To have an endless supply of different napkin rings at your fingertips, invest in a selection of braids, cords and ribbons from a haberdasher. Don't underestimate how much you'll need – allow a good 40cm of cord or braid for each napkin. Wind your chosen cord generously round a rolled napkin – two or three times is best – and finish with a plain knot. To make a napkin ring of wide pleated ribbon, allow 20cm of ribbon and wrap it round the rolled napkin then add contrasting silver cord and tie in a smart knot to hold the ribbon securely in place. For a lavish, extra frilly effect, use twice as much ribbon and wrap it round in a double layer.

Opposite: Candleholders made from pleated metallic ribbon wrapped round a glass votive or jam jar ideally complement silver table mats.

Left: Jars, vases or other candleholders can be transformed by a surround of pleated metallic paper. You'll get best results with straight-sided containers.

contemporary candles

Candles add instant style to a table. Increase their impact with unusual containers and imaginative presentation for the contemporary Christmas table.

Pleated and corrugated paper and ribbon can also be used to transform plain glass jars or vases into elegant candleholders at minimal cost. Choose ribbon that is slightly deeper than the votive holder you want to cover. Cut a length of ribbon to the circumference of the holder, wrap the ribbon around and glue or tape in place. Use candles that are lower in height than their container and never leave them burning unattended. Paper can also be used to disguise jars or candlesticks. Cut a piece of paper to the required height and twice the circumference of the container. Fold the paper every 2cm to form pleats. Wrap it loosely around the container – if you pull too tight, you'll destroy the pleats.

Vases, tins, jars and glasses can all be pressed into service as candle-holders. Once they have been covered with paper or ribbon, no one need know what is underneath.

Before you get busy with paper, scissors and glue, take a minute to consider the intended setting for your candles and holders. A row of short candles is better suited to a long narrow dinner table than one large candle in the centre, while on a side table, a group of candles of varying height will add more interest than one sole candle. However, a round table works well with one large single candle or a cluster of candles placed in the centre. Vases, tins, jars and drinking glasses can all be pressed into service as different sized candleholders. Once they have been covered with a layer of pretty paper or a length of glittery ribbon, no one need know what is underneath.

Right: Wrap small glasses, jars or votive holders with silver or gold crepe paper so that, when lit, the candle within casts a mellow glow. Make sure that you cut a piece of paper that is slightly taller than the container and wider than its circumference. Fold over any raw edges and glue the overlap neatly in place.

Left: Use corrugated paper to disguise flower vases and turn them into contemporary candle-holders. Fill tall vases with gravel to within 5cm of the rim; place the candle on top and pack more gravel around the candle to hold it securely in place. If you've left it too late to buy gravel or stones, raid the kitchen cupboard and use rice instead.

65

hanging lanterns

Paper lanterns make perfect Christmas decorations and are so easy to make. If you don't have a mantelpiece to dress festively, string a group of lanterns in a front window to welcome visitors.

Paper lanterns couldn't be simpler to make, but if you don't feel confident start by practising on some scrap paper. Fold a sheet of A4 paper in half lengthways. Every 1.5cm or so, make a cut through the fold, stopping about 1.5cm from the top edges. Unfold the paper and roll it into a cylinder, overlap the edges and glue them together. Thread a darning needle with thin cord and stitch a loop to hang the lantern from. You can create variations by using different weights of paper and different patterns. To add interest, vary the heights and sizes of the lanterns and glue scraps of sequinned braids or ribbons around the tops and bottoms.

Opposite and left: These lanterns have been cut from a selection of silver and gold patterned papers and hung with glittery thread at a window. Some have been embellished further with strips of furnishing braid glued to the top and bottom rims.

Left: Tinsel banding contrasts with silvery twigs.

Below: Beaded Christmas-tree trim can be used in the same way for a sparkling, glittering effect.

Right: Christmas-tree stars gain a new lease of life when fixed at intervals around the wreath.

silver wreath

Take one ready-made twig wreath and dress it in three different ways to create a glittering contemporary decoration ideal for a front door or wall.

First of all you need to spray the twig wreath with silver paint. You will get a better finish if you apply several thin coats of paint rather than trying to cover the wreath in one go. When the paint has dried completely, decorate the wreath using one of three techniques: use a glue gun to attach Christmas tree stars at intervals around the wreath; wrap the wreath with a neat spiral of good old-fashioned tinsel and glue the ends in place; or twist beaded Christmas tree braid round it in a similar fashion.

A ready-made twig wreath provides a
versatile base for a glittering silvery wreath
that can be redecorated every year.

country christmas

Christmas in the country is a relaxed family affair, traditional yet fuss-free, using materials gathered from the garden and the hedgerow to create an informal rustic setting for the festivities. Berries and greenery, antique linens and church candles all have their part to play in creating a simple red and creamy white scheme.

Opposite: A bough of crab apples (above left) forms a simple centrepiece for this country Christmas table, with candles arranged at intervals along each side. Antique linen tea towels make perfect place mats, while napkin rings are formed from flexible birch twigs and a spray of snowberries (above right).

70

table settings and decorations

Berries and fruit of all kinds can be used to create festive table

settings. Choose from pearly snowberries, rosy crab apples or scarlet

rowan berries – provided the birds haven't got there first! If bushes

are bare, very realistic-looking artificial berries are now available.

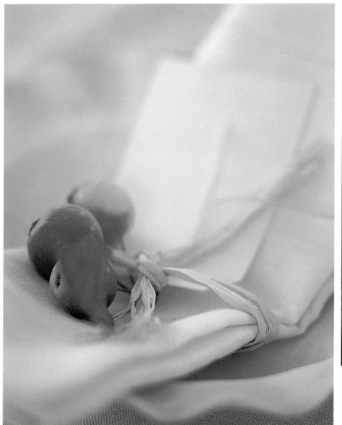

Far left: A folded napkin is tied with raffia and a cluster of crab apples.

Left: A mini galvanized metal bucket is filled with berries and autumn leaves, but you could substitute ivy or a sprig of holly.

Opposite and below: Tie napkins with flexible twigs (thin birch twigs are ideal) then tuck in a sprig of evergreen foliage and snowberries. Arrange the napkins in a basket with pine cones and greenery.

Below: For a glowing ball of light, fill a galvanized metal bucket or a similar container with sand then firmly push in beeswax tapers. Place in a window or porch to greet visitors.

Right: The enamel basin belonging to this old washstand is the ideal home for a display of larger candles. Alternatively, you could buy a new enamel basin and place it on the floor or a side table.

Opposite below and detail: Many decorations are surprisingly versatile. Here, a berried wreath doubles up as a candle surround.

country candles

Candlelight is mellow, intimate and magical, and lit candles will bring an immediately festive atmosphere to any room. Stand candles on mantelpieces, mass them on windowsills or position them in the centre of the table. Remember that candles make more impact when they are used *en masse*, so be generous with quantities.

A foliage, berry and fruit wreath makes a bold table centrepiece or a welcoming arrangement in a hallway. Ready-made wreath bases made from florists' foam are available in various sizes, as are circular plastic frames that hold the wreath and protect the surface beneath. Submerge the foam and frame in a bowl of water; when it stops bubbling, the foam is wet through and ready to use. Randomly push short lengths of foliage and sprays of berries into the wreath, letting them spill generously over the sides to conceal the plastic frame. To make a stem for the apples, firmly push a length of florists' wire through the base of the fruit. Bring the two ends of the wire together and twist tightly into a stem. Push the wire stems deep into the foam to hold the apple in position. Finally, place the candles in the centre and light.

A row of candles on a windowsill greets visitors with a festive sight.

Opposite and below: An idea of utter simplicity and great charm. Thick glass jam jars double up as nightlights, each adorned with a twist of variegated ivy, whose glossy leaves catch the candlelight. Wrap the ivy tightly just below the rim of the jam jars and secure by twisting the ends together – use a piece of wire if necessary.

Opposite: The simplest arrangements suit an informal country setting. An armful of stems loosely massed in a well-worn bucket harmonizes well with scrubbed floorboards and modest furnishings. Mistletoe would make a good alternative, with its pretty foliage and near-translucent berries arranged in a cascade tumbling towards the floor. **Below:** Continue the foliage theme on a festive table by winding lengths of ivy around water glasses.

decorative foliage

Decorating the house with greenery at the bleakest time of year is a tradition that dates back to pagan times. Even today we still appreciate the cheerful colour and form of evergreens during winter when most other plants are dormant.

This Christmas, why not break away from traditional holly, mistletoe and pine cones and look for alternative foliage and berries to deck the halls with? It's surprising what you can find, even in a small city garden – look out for shiny black viburnum berries, waxy snowberries or rosehips in different shapes and sizes – any plants with brightly coloured berries and glossy, prettily shaped evergreen leaves are ideal. Whatever you collect from the great outdoors, keep your arrangements deliberately casual. Use rustic, country-style containers – galvanized metal buckets, jam jars or plain enamel jugs – rather than fine crystal or china vases.

Greenery and berries make stunningly simple Christmas decorations, and it's amazing how much you can find in your own garden.

Right: A cream-glazed earthenware milk jug is the perfect foil for a bunch of freshly cut, heavily berried viburnum (*Viburnum tinus*). Other good garden plants for berries include pyracantha – which has the drawback of being rather spiky – and cotoneaster, which has fiery foliage as its leaves die. The chocolate boxes beneath this arrangement are tied with raffia and a spray of hops.

Country hedgerows may yield skeins of old man's beard (a type of wild clematis), wild hops and climbing bryony with jewel-like translucent red berries, all of which can be used for eye-catchingly different decorations. Even hops bought from florists or dried flower specialists will still retain a pretty tinge of green.

Left: A generous hank of green hops tied with a loop of cheery gingham ribbon makes a stunningly simple front door decoration.

Below: An elegantly spare circlet of snowberry leaves is wound on to a thin wire hoop and held in place with florist's wire.

cookies and candles

For a country Christmas, choose a simple theme for your tree. Star-shaped cookies and real candles are a modest combination that nevertheless possesses great charm and is extremely effective.

Once the only way of lighting your tree, real candles are making a comeback and special spring-clip candleholders are available in shops and department stores. Always remember to keep candles well away from other tree decorations and never leave the room while they are burning. Edible tree decorations are another well-established tradition. Cookie cutters come in all shapes and sizes, so experiment with different themes – hearts, Christmas trees or gingerbread snowmen. If you are handy with an icing gun, try embellishing shapes with icing-sugar details. Old-fashioned royal icing, made from icing sugar and egg white, which hardens to a shiny finish, is ideal. Place your tree in a large container and allow plenty of space for presents underneath.

Opposite and above: Spicy star-shaped cookies suspended from loops of pretty gingham ribbon make inexpensive Christmas decorations with a decidedly countrified feel (see recipe on next page).

To make a hole to thread the ribbon through, pierce each cookie with a skewer, 1cm from the edge, before you put them in the oven. The evocative scent of cloves and ginger adds to the festive atmosphere.

83

Right: As well as decorating the tree, spiced cookies – plain or iced – are a novel way of decorating a present. Thread a cookie on a piece of string and tie this to a longer length of ribbon to tie up the parcel.

SPICED STAR COOKIES

150g unsalted butter, softened

175g caster sugar

1 medium egg, lightly beaten

250g plain flour

½ teaspoon baking powder

¼ teaspoon bicarbonate of soda

½ teaspoon ground ginger

½ teaspoon ground cloves

½ teaspoon ground allspice

Makes 25 cookies

1 Cream the butter and sugar together until pale and fluffy. Beat in the egg, a little at a time, until thoroughly mixed.

2 Sift the flour, baking powder, bicarbonate of soda and spices into a bowl, then stir into the egg mixture. Bring together to form a soft dough, wrap in clingfilm and chill for at least 1 hour.

3 Knead the dough to soften, then roll out to 5mm thick. Cut out stars using an 8cm star-shaped biscuit cutter. Gather the trimmings, re-roll, then stamp out more stars. Put them 2cm apart on lightly greased baking sheets. Using a skewer, make a small hole in each star about 1cm from the edge.

4 Bake in a preheated oven at 180°C (350°F) Gas 4 for 10–15 minutes. Remove from the oven and let cool on the baking sheets then transfer to a wire rack. When cold, thread ribbon through the holes and tie or store in an airtight container.

cards & decorations

Far right: To make a cut-out card, cut a long rectangle of thick paper and mark three equal sections. Score along each section and fold. Lay the piece of card on a cutting mat and, using a stencil, cut out your motif from the middle section. Glue a piece of gold paper behind the cut out then fold over one third of the card and glue so it conceals the gold paper.

Above: Using thick artist's paper (watercolour paper is ideal) cut out two rectangles 21cm x 15cm. Fold each piece in half and make two holes, 3.5cm from top and bottom, on each fold. Lay one card on top of the other and thread the holes with ribbon, tying it in a bow. Collect dried leaves, spray them with silver paint, then glue a leaf to every other side of the card.

Right: Cut a long rectangle, again from thick textured artist's paper, and fold it in half. Cut a series of five-pointed stars from metallic paper (leftover wrapping paper will do). Glue them in a line across the centre of the card, then place a smaller star within each. Stationers sell packets of gummed silver and gold stars that are ideal for this purpose.

handmade cards

Handmade cards are so much more personal than shop-bought ones and they
need not be too difficult or time-consuming to make. Using just a few simple
tools and techniques, scraps and oddments of rich fabrics, glittery braids,
silky ribbons and pretty paper can be transformed into stylish cards – the
imaginative and unusual results are bound to become treasured keepsakes.

Right: Turn a shutter or door into a festive gallery. Cut a length of ribbon to fit shutter or door panel and secure with blu-tac or drawing pins. Use paper clips to attach cards.
Below: If you like to re-read cards, arrange them in a toast rack. Change the order daily to vary the display.

Opposite: Use these basic tips to create a variety of handmade cards. Start by cutting out cards in thick watercolour paper to your chosen size. Cut decorative shapes, such as stars, holly sprigs, Christmas trees or bells from pretty paper or coloured felt (an ideal fabric because it doesn't fray). Glue the shape to the card and decorate further, if desired, by sticking on sequins or glitter. Or try gluing ribbon remnants to a card in the shape of a cross and filling in the gaps with ready-gummed gold and silver stars.

Decorate handmade cards with Christmassy shapes cut from coloured felt – an ideal fabric because it doesn't fray.

Left and below: Find new and imaginative ways to display your Christmas cards. This greetings tree is made from tall branches of contorted willow that have been stood upright in a container – use scrunched up newspaper, coarse sand or pebbles to hold them in position. The Christmas cards are attached to the branches with neat cord or ribbon loops, which have been fastened to each card with a paper clip. For other unusual display ideas, see also the ribbon gallery on the previous page.

christmas stockings

Colourful handmade children's Christmas stockings can be used year after year and fast become favourite treasures, eagerly awaited when the decorations are unpacked every December.

Felt is the best fabric for Christmas stockings: it doesn't fray and comes in a rainbow of colours. Cut out a paper template for the stocking (it's best to be generous – it's easy to inadvertently make them too small). Then cut out two stocking shapes. Decorate the front of one shape, leaving the other piece plain. Place the two shapes together, decorated side up, and sew, using a simple running stitch.

Left and right: When decorating each stocking, use your imagination. Buttons can become balloons while sequins double up as Christmas tree baubles. Cut squares of felt for parcels and use the stitches that join them to the stocking to represent string.

alternative tree toppers

No Christmas tree is properly dressed until it has its tree topper in place. Choose a generously sized ready-made sequinned star like the one shown below or – even better – make your own dazzling decoration that will last for years to come.

Above: Cut four strips of card, 25cm long and 1.5cm wide. Glue metallic ribbon of the same length and width to each strip. Let them dry, then glue strips of narrow sequinned braid down the top of each strip. When dry, arrange the strips to form an eight-pointed star and secure each one at the point where they cross using strong glue. Use a piece of florist's wire to fasten the star to the tree.

Right: Customize bought decorations to make tree toppers. Two holes have been pierced in the back of this sequinned star, and a length of florist's wire has been threaded through to hold the star to the tree.

Left: To make this picture-bow topper you will need about 1.4m of metallic ribbon with wired edges and a length of florist's wire. Cut the ribbon into two lengths measuring 65cm and 75cm. Fold the longer piece into a loop and overlap the two ends at the loop's centre back. Fold the shorter piece in two and place it behind the first loop to form a cross. Wrap florist's wire tightly round the centre of the cross to form a large bow. Use the ends of the wire to fasten the bow to the tree. Trim the ends of the ribbon and arrange the bow.

tree decorations

It's a Christmas ritual; the moment when the box

of decorations is brought down from the attic or

the top of the wardrobe. By adding both handmade

and shop-bought decorations every year, you'll

soon build up a collection of family heirlooms.

Above left: Miniature parcels for the Christmas tree can be made by covering stock or bouillon cubes with scraps of wrapping paper and snippets of ribbon. To create a range of shapes, try wrapping up match boxes too or even making your own tiny boxes from cardboard.

Above right: This tiny flowerpot filled with miniature baubles is easy to make and is decidedly superior to the average bauble. Give tiny terracotta pots (from craft shops) a coat of gold spray paint. Fill them with scrunched up tissue paper and glue gold beads over the surface (using a glue gun makes life much easier). To hang them on the tree, glue a length of narrow ribbon to the base of the pot and again close to the rim and tie in a loop.

Left: Remnants of brocade and embroidered fabrics can be turned into elegant bags to decorate the tree. Simply cut a rectangle of fabric and fold it right sides together. Stitch two sides closed, turn the right way out and hem the top opening. Fill bags with spicy pot-pourri or a couple of sugared almonds, or fake it with a tissue-paper filling. Then tie the neck with a scrap of ribbon.

Christmas decorations are now big business and it's no longer a seasonal trade – some Christmas shops stay open all year round. So there's every opportunity to build up a treasured collection of glittery baubles and other trinkets. Once you've amassed many different tree decorations, you can play it two ways. Either mix and match baubles, stuffed and embroidered shapes, beaded decorations and Indian wirework ornaments for an eclectic, global look. Alternatively, choose a theme each year and use just part of your collection. A single colour could be a starting point, or you might choose a particular shape or motif as the basis for a decorating theme.

Opposite: Modern decorations imported from India resemble old heirloom ornaments and bring an air of antiquity to the tree.
Left: Fragile glass baubles may fade and become tarnished with age, but that's all part of their appeal. Store them in a box with cardboard dividers or in eggboxes to prolong their life.
Above: Elaborate metallic openwork globes can form the basis for a silver and gold decorating theme.

Baubles, beading and tinsel are only the starting point for a collection of Christmas decorations. More and more ornaments come onto the market every year, allowing you to add to your treasure chest of decorations. Look out for unusual wooden figures, paper ornaments and other novel decorations at Christmas craft markets and fairs: a great many are made in Eastern Europe, though some come from as far away as Sri Lanka, India and Japan.

Above: Intricately folded tissue-paper shapes are perennially popular. Traditional forms include bells, fruits, snowmen and coloured globes. They fold flat when not in use and the soft wire catches that hold them open tend to need reinforcing with tape after a few years.

Right: Wooden decorations are ideal for families with small children as they are more robust than baubles. Naive painted santas, clowns and snowmen are particularly charming.

Opposite: This glittery festive elephant adorned with frills and fancy ribbons is an Indian stuffed-cloth tree decoration. Why not collect a whole menagerie of animals? Look out for fish bristling with gold sequin scales, embroidered cats and red plush camels.

Look out for unusual wooden figures, paper ornaments and other novel decorations at Christmas craft markets.

wrapping & gifts

giftwrapping ideas

Imaginatively wrapped presents can be just as much a part of the
Christmas setting as the tree they are piled under. Adding ribbon is
one of the easiest and most stylish ways to dress up a parcel.

Left: Old-fashioned pill boxes make perfect containers for special presents such as earrings or cufflinks. There's no need to wrap the box – simply tie with ribbon.

Opposite: French paper sweet bags make pretty giftwrapping. Place the gift inside, roll the top down and punch two holes through the rolled paper. Thread with ribbon and tie.

Above: To make a gift bag, use a 'mould' such as a book. Wrap a length of good-quality paper around the book and tape the central join, then neatly fold and tape one end. Slip the book out and crease the narrow sides to form a bag shape. Place the gift inside, fold over the top edge twice, then wrap ribbon around the bag and tie.

107

While gift vouchers or money are often welcome presents, handing over a plain white envelope shows a distinct lack of imagination.

While gift vouchers or money are often welcome presents, handing over a plain white envelope shows a distinct lack of imagination. Instead, disguise vouchers or notes in rolled tubes, which can be embellished in many ways. Cut squares of card, lay the voucher (in its envelope) on top and roll up tightly. Tape in place, wrap and tie with a ribbon.

Opposite: This selection of beaded hat pins came from an antiques market. Tie them to the gift tubes with a length of gauzy ribbon (**above**) or use one to fasten a conventionally wrapped present, remembering to replace the safety cap on the pin.
Left: If you have several gift vouchers to give, pile the decorated tubes in a pretty bowl or add an extra ribbon loop and hang them from the tree.

*Finish off a smartly wrapped parcel
with a sparkly decoration or a sumptuous
embroidered ribbon, tied in a jaunty bow.*

Right: Gold is the theme for a trio of parcels wrapped in shiny metallics.

Below: A pile of presents are linked by a common colour theme but are wrapped in papers that couldn't be more different in terms of texture.

Above: A sequinned, star-shaped Christmas tree decoration adds a glittery finishing touch to a smartly wrapped parcel, and gives someone two presents in one.

Above: Layering paper and ribbon is a particularly pretty way to wrap gifts. Wrap a broad strip of paper around the box or package, then place a narrower layer of paper or ribbon on top. Finish off with a sumptuous embroidered ribbon, tied in a jaunty bow.

candles

Candles make ideal gifts at a time of year when candlelight plays an important part in creating a festive atmosphere. Pretty wrappings can transform these inexpensive gifts into desirable luxuries.

Opulent wrapping papers and rich silks give candles added impact. By embellishing simple votive glasses and tying bundles of candles with an extravagant swathe of gauze or silk ribbon, you can create such a pretty effect that it would be wasted effort to wrap them any further. Far better to let the candles themselves be part of the decoration. Be warned – keep tall thin candles away from radiators or fires as they will warp in the heat.

Right: Personalize a candle in a plain glass votive by adding a band of ribbon, lightly fixed with glue, and a girdle of silky cord.

Opposite: A bundle of slim tapers bound in pleated silk and secured with a contrasting ribbon bow makes an irresistible gift.

Embellish votive glasses and bundles of candles with an extravagant swathe of silky ribbon to create a pretty effect.

Right: Rustic beeswax candles smell almost good enough to eat. Wrap them in an old-fashioned paper doily and tie with an elegantly ruffled ribbon for a welcome and useful gift.

Above and above left: Old teacups that have lost their matching saucers make pretty candleholders. You'll need some paraffin wax, available from craft shops in solid blocks or pellet form, and a length of wick. Melt the wax in a basin over a pan of simmering water (never melt over direct heat). Cut a length of wick and tie one end to a pencil. Rest the pencil on the cup so that the wick is hanging in the centre, and pour in the hot wax. When set, trim the wick.
Below left: Use the same technique to fill gold-painted flowerpots, first blocking drainage holes with blu-tac.

Making your own sweetly
scented gifts couldn't
be simpler, as
these lavender
bags prove.

scented gifts

Scented presents are traditional Christmas gifts, whether they are

a bar of luxury soap, a phial of precious perfume or foaming potions

for the bath. And making your own sweetly scented gifts couldn't

be simpler, as these pot-pourri sachets and lavender bags prove.

Opposite: No sewing required. Just place a handful of delicately scented pot-pourri or a bar of soap in the centre of an antique handkerchief, scoop up the edges and catch them with a ribbon in a coordinated colour.

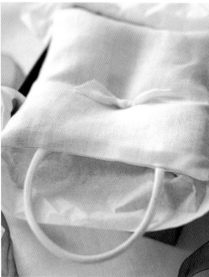

Above and left: Traditional lavender bags are given extra seasonal relevance when trimmed with a Christmas tree decoration. This pretty idea also works well for scented bath salts, but first put them in a plastic bag so they don't seep through the fabric.

117

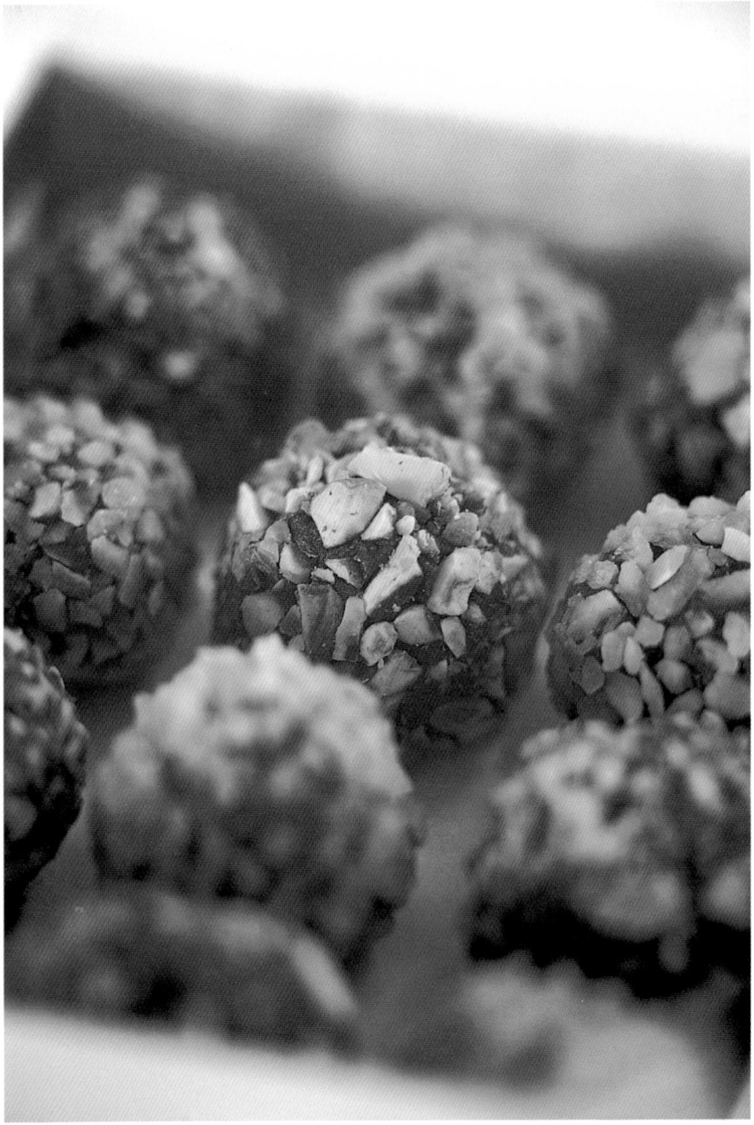

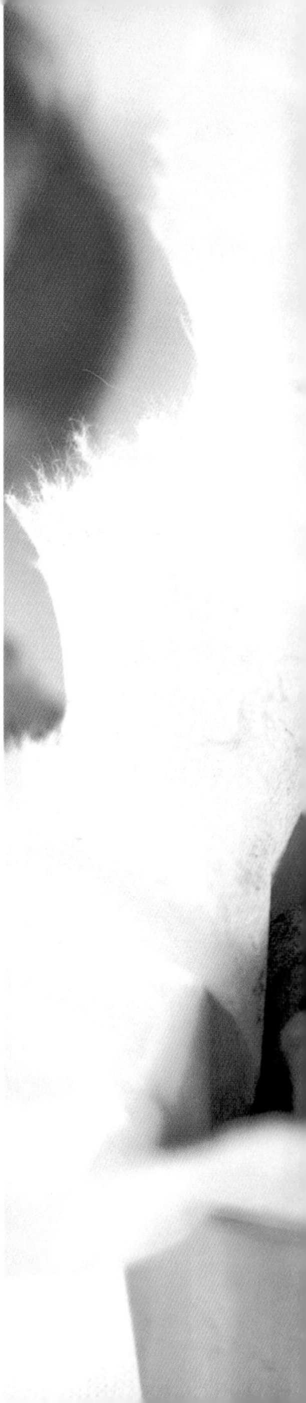

edible treats

Gourmets are sure to appreciate a box or basket of the most indulgent home-made chocolates, made only from the finest ingredients.

The time and effort that go into home-made presents show friends and family how much you care. Chocolates are not complicated and are fun to make. One basic recipe (see next page) can be adapted to suit several different tastes – by rolling finished sweets in chopped nuts, dusting them in cocoa powder or decorating them with glacé fruits, for example. Containers for home-made chocolates can include simple paper cones, small boxes lined with handmade paper, miniature carrier bags or even small wooden punnets.

Left and opposite: Home-made gifts will always be appreciated more than bought ones because of the thought, time and effort that they represent.

119

Indulgent, rich and delicious, home-made chocolate truffles are the perfect gift — not least because they are so easy to make!

CHOCOLATE TRUFFLES

25g raisins	**For the coating:**
1 tablespoon rum	50g unsweetened cocoa powder
25g caster sugar	75g chopped nuts, such as pistachios
25g unblanched hazelnuts	or almonds
200g good-quality plain chocolate	100g good-quality plain chocolate
50g unsalted butter	25g good-quality white chocolate
150ml double cream	
1 tablespoon brandy	Makes 27 truffles in total

1 Put the raisins in a small bowl, add the rum, cover and leave to soak overnight.

2 Lightly oil a baking sheet. Put the sugar and hazelnuts in a small, heavy-based saucepan and heat gently until the sugar has melted and starts to caramelize. Boil until golden brown, then pour onto the baking sheet and let set. When hard, break the praline into pieces and crush to a coarse powder.

3 Melt the chocolate and butter in a heatproof bowl over a pan of simmering water, then stir in the cream. Let cool for 1 hour.

4 Divide the truffle mixture into three bowls: add the brandy to one, the rum-soaked raisins to the second and the praline to the third. Let set in the refrigerator overnight.

5 For the rum and raisin truffles, sift the cocoa powder into a bowl, add teaspoonfuls of the truffle mixture, one at a time, and toss gently to coat.

6 For the brandy truffles, shape teaspoonfuls of the truffle mixture into balls, then roll in the chopped pistachios or almonds until completely covered.

7 For the praline truffles, melt the plain chocolate then, using a fork, dip small balls of the truffle mixture into the chocolate to coat and shake off any excess. Put the truffle balls on baking parchment to set. Melt the white chocolate and drizzle over the truffles. Leave to set.

8 Store the truffles in the refrigerator for up to 1 week.

Above and right: Perfect presentation: these praline truffles have been casually drizzled with melted white chocolate, placed in tiny individual paper cases and arranged on a dainty glass cake stand.

This page and opposite: If you don't have time to bake your own gifts, such as the cheese straws opposite, then buy some delicious biscuits and repackage them more imaginatively, in pretty paper-lined boxes, for example, tied with ribbon.

CHEESE TWISTS

500g ready-made puff pastry
3 tablespoons wholegrain mustard
75g mature cheddar cheese, grated
25g freshly grated Parmesan cheese

Makes 36 twists

1 On a lightly floured surface, roll out the pastry to a rectangle, about 16cm x 40cm. With the short edge facing you, spread 1½ tablespoons of the mustard over the top two-thirds of the pastry, leaving a 1-cm border around the edges. Sprinkle half of the cheeses on top of the mustard and press down gently.

2 Fold the uncovered bottom third of the pastry up over half the cheese, then carefully fold down the top third. Seal in the cheese by pressing the open sides firmly with a rolling pin.

3 Give the pastry a quarter turn. Repeat the rolling and folding process using the remaining mustard and cheeses.

4 Roll out the pastry to a rectangle, about 26cm x 34cm. Trim the edges. Cut into strips, about 1.5cm x 17cm and twist into spirals. Put 2cm apart on greased baking sheets and bake in a preheated oven at 200°C (400°F) Gas 6 for 15–20 minutes until puffed and golden.

5 Remove from the oven and let cool on the baking sheets for 5 minutes, then transfer to a wire rack to cool completely. Store in an airtight container or freeze for up to 1 month.

SPICED NUTS

200g each of blanched almonds,
hazelnuts and cashew nuts
1 tablespoon olive oil
½ teaspoon garlic salt
2 teaspoons jerk seasoning (this is
available from larger supermarkets or
from Caribbean grocers)

1 Put the nuts in a large bowl, add the olive oil and mix. Sprinkle the salt and jerk seasoning over and mix thoroughly.

2 Spread the nuts on a baking sheet and bake in a preheated oven at 180°C (350°F) Gas 4 for 12–15 minutes until browned. Cool, then store in an airtight container.

Makes 600g of spiced nuts in total

If you are holding a party, leave a gift at each place setting. Alternatively, arrange small packages under the tree or hand to guests as they depart.

Home-made delicacies packed in imaginative containers look far more stylish than shop-bought foods. Unusual fabrics make pretty covers for jam-jar lids, and cellophane bags are ideal for nuts and other oily foods or buttery biscuits and truffles. If you plan to package biscuits or chocolates in handmade paper or cardboard boxes, line them with greaseproof or waxed paper to stop oil seeping through. There's no right or wrong way to give presents. If you are holding a party, leave a gift at each place setting. Alternatively, arrange small packages beneath the tree or hand to guests as they depart.

Above left: A wooden punnet like the ones strawberries are sometimes sold in is lined with Japanese paper then used to hold home-made biscuits. A gingham ribbon completes the look.
Left: Repackage olives from the deli counter in a glass jar and top up with olive oil. The cap is made from a square of greaseproof paper topped with a scrap of open-weave fabric and held in place by a festive gold cord.
Opposite: Spiced nuts bagged in cellophane make perfect going-home gifts after a Christmas party.

stockists

CHRISTMAS DECORATIONS

Most department stores have a good selection of Christmas decorations, but the following stores and shops are particularly good.

The Christmas Shop
Hays Galleria
55a Tooley Street
London SE1 2QN
(020) 7378 1998
Open all year round.

The General Trading Company
144 Sloane Street
London SW1X 9BL
(020) 7730 0411

Graham & Green
4, 7 & 10 Elgin Crescent
London W11 2JA
(020) 7727 4594

Harrods
Knightsbridge
SW1X 7XL
(020) 7730 1234
Their Christmas department opens in August.

Liberty
214–220 Regent Street
London W1R 6AH
(020) 7734 1234

Selfridges
400 Oxford Street
London W1A 1AB
(020) 7629 1234

Shaker
72–73 Marylebone High St
London W1M 3AR
(020) 7935 9461
Phone for mail order details.

Tobias and the Angel
66 White Hart Lane
London SW13 0PZ
(020) 8878 8902
Handmade decorations as well as old and antique decorations.

The Traditional Christmas Shop
High Street
Lechlade
Gloucestershire GL7 3AD
(01367) 253184
Open all year.

RIBBONS AND TRIMMINGS

The Bead Shop
21a Tower Street
London WC2H 9NS
(020) 7240 0931

Camden Passage Antiques Market
Islington, London N1
Wednesday and Saturday until 3pm only. Good for old ribbons and trimmings.

Ells & Farrier
20 Beak Street
London W1R 3HA
(020) 7629 9964
Over 3,000 types of beads as well as feathers, sequins and glittery trimmings.

V.V. Rouleaux
54 Sloane Square
London SW1W 8AX
(020) 7730 3125
also at
6 Marylebone High Street
London W1M 3PB
(020) 7224 5179
The ultimate ribbon shop.

John Lewis Partnership
Oxford Street
London W1A 1EX
(020) 7629 7711

Liberty
see under Christmas
decorations for address.

Paperchase
213 Tottenham Court Road
London W1P 9AF
(020) 7580 8496
This store has a special
Christmas department. Call
(0161) 839 1500 for details of
other stores and mail order.

PAPER AND CARD
Most art shops and stationers
have a good supply of paper
and card as well as other
useful items such as glitter,
coloured pens, glue, etc.

Atlantis
146 Brick Lane
London E1 6RU
(020) 7377 8855
Probably Europe's largest art
materials store. Excellent if
you want to buy in bulk

Falkiner Fine Papers
76 Southampton Row
London WC1B 4AR
(020) 7831 1151
A wonderful selection of
handmade paper; particularly
good for lacy Japanese papers
and metallic papers.

Paperchase
A fantastic selection of paper
and card. See under Ribbons
and trimmings for address.

CANDLES

Angelic
194 King's Road
London SW3 5ED
(020) 7351 1557
Call (020) 7267 9299 for
details of their numerous
other stores.

Candlemaking Supplies
28 Blythe Road
London W14 0HA
(020) 7602 4031/2
This shop contains everything
you need to make candles as
well as offering a huge choice
of candles for sale. Catalogue
and mail order available.

Organics
98 Ravenscroft Road
London E2
Part of the famous Columbia
Road flower market. Open
8am–2pm, Sundays only.

Price's Candles
110 York Road
London SW11 3RU
(020) 7801 2030

CHRISTMAS TREES

While it is convenient to buy
your tree from a local garden
centre or market, it's more
fun to visit an out-of-town
Christmas tree grower where
a 'choose and cut' system is
offered. For details of growers
in your area, contact The
British Christmas Tree Growers
Association (0131) 447 0499.

acknowledgments

Firstly I would like to say a big thank you to everyone at Ryland Peters & Small who has worked so hard to produce *Christmas Details*: Alison Starling, Gabriella Le Grazie, Megan Smith, Sally Powell and Kate Brunt. A special thank you goes to my editor, Annabel Morgan, for her constant enthusiasm and support throughout the deluge of baubles and tinsel. Also thanks to Kathy Man for all the festive cooking. Many, many thanks to my wonderful assistant, Kirsten Robinson, not just for her efficiency but also for her cheerfulness and keenness throughout. Thank you to Sandra Lane for her beautiful pictures and to her assistant Claudia Dulak. I would also like to thank my agent, Fiona Lindsay. As always, my husband has been constantly supportive, and wisely took work in Rio during the many weeks of Christmas upheaval here at home. A huge thank you.

The photographs on pages 2 and 44–48 are by Debi Treloar.

The author and publisher would like to thank Stephan Schulte and Sheila Scholes for allowing them to photograph in their homes.